LIFE ACCORDING TO MOTOWN

Patricia Smith

TIA CHUCHA PRESS
CHICAGO

ACKNOWLEDGMENTS

Thanks to Marc Smith, Luis Rodriguez and Michael Warr for the laughter, unflinching support and enduring friendship; to Gwendolyn Brooks, the undisputed queen of the colored girl; and to my hometown Chicago, with its bright lights and incomparable audiences.

And my arms are forever open to my husband Bruce, my son Damon and the incomparable Mikaila, the trio who transformed me through love.

Printed in the United States

ISBN 978-0-9624287-2-2

Book design: Jane Brunette

Published by:
Tia Chucha Press
A Project of Tia Chucha's Centro Cultural, Inc.
PO Box 328
San Fernando, CA 91341
www.tiachucha.com

Distributed by:
Northwestern University Press
Chicago Distribution Center
11030 South Langley Avenue
Chicago, IL 606028

Tia Chucha Press is the publishing wing of Tia Chucha's Centro Cultural, Inc., a 501 (c) 3 non-profit corporation. Tia Chucha's Centro Cultural has received funding for this book from the National Endowment for the Arts. Other funding for Tia Chucha's Centro Cultural's programming and operations has come from the California Arts Council, Los Angeles County Arts Commission, Los Angeles City Department of Cultural Affairs, The California Community Foundation, the Annenberg Foundation, the Weingart Foundation, National Association of Latino Arts and Culture, Ford Foundation, MetLife, Southwest Airlines, the Andy Warhol Foundation for the Visual Arts, the Thrill Hill Foundation, the Middleton Foundation, Center for Cultural Innovation, Not Just Us Foundation, John Irvine Foundation, and The Guacamole Fund, among others. Donations have also come from Bruce Springsteen, John Densmore of the Doors, Jackson Browne, Lou Adler, Richard Foos, Adrienne Rich, Tom Hayden, Dave Marsh, Mel Gilman, Jack Kornfield, Jesus Trevino, David Sandoval, Gary Stewart, Denise Chavez and John Randall of the Border Book Festival, and Luis & Trini Rodriguez, as well as others.

CONTENTS

To my father, Otis Douglas Smith,
who left me here to tend his light..

PREFACE

Oh Mary Mac, Mac Mac
All dressed in black, black, black
With silver buttons, buttons, buttons
All down her back, back, back.
She asked her mother, mother, mother
For fifteen cents, cents, cents
To see the elephant, elephant, elephant
Jump the fence, fence, fence.
He jumped so high, high, high
He touched the sky, sky, sky
And he didn't come back, back, back
Till the fourth of July, ly, ly.

●WHEN I WAS EIGHT YEARS OLD, a child of southern folk, I could hurtle through inherited rhythms. I was obsessed with clapping games, the hand jive, I could whip a revolution with my fingers. Smack, pat, clap, clap, snap, telling rhythmic tall tales of little girls and flying elephants—and blue-black superheroes who only flew on Fridays, because—as everybody knows—that's when the eagle flew. The twins, Karen and Kathy Ford, were better at rapidfiring the rhymes, but I could make my hands a blur without ever losing it. I sewed those buttons down Mary Mac's blackside. That dime and nickel also glittered in my fist.

I was a first daughter. Asked to create our own histories, we taught our hands to sing, and they grew callused with necessary music. Those songs we slapped were the first step in learning where our souls were, the place where our histories could actually begin. Swathed in Chi-soul, we were born knowing about the singing out. But it was eight years before I knew about the singing in—how we need to pull lyrics and backbeats and plump single notes into ourselves and hold them there.

Once you learn the location of the soul, you must immediately begin to feed it.

My whole body yearned for sound. Because I spent so much time inside, alone with my books and rampant imagination, I assumed folks were singing about what I wasn't seeing. I heard whole stories in guitar riffs, sax solos, finger pops. I held onto lyrics for dear life. I already knew that words and their music had the muscle to save me.

Motown was the muscle. My poetry sprang directly from the targeted lyrics, the perfect brown throats of smooth crooners. As I grew up on the West Side of Chicago, it was my soundtrack. All my beliefs about what held my life together came from the sweet spin of a 45 on a clunky old phonograph. When I became a woman, my yesterdays were still firmly rooted in the soul of songs. There was only one place for my poetry to begin.

The poems in *Life According to Motown* comprise a snapshot of my life at the time I lived it. They're an outloud rendering of vulnerabilities, triumphs, revelations, secrets, insecurities, rebirths, persistent music and, yes—quite a few missteps.

I flip through the pages of this book—after a lifetime of sweating my work forward—and I wish I could change every word. I see opportunities to spark lyricism, places where I tiptoed around the heart of a poem and avoided the real truth, times when I rushed the narrative in order to get the work to a stage. This is the work of a young and impetuous woman, a woman just discovering the irresistible dangers of verb and noun. Now that I've studied structure and theory, now that I see so many beginnings that never reached a satisfying end, I'd love to re-examine the pulse and muscle of each poem. I want to rebuild, revise, re-create. I see a thousand new ways to make the poems sing.

That said, I wouldn't change a damned thing. Everything I was found a place between these covers. Here is the gangly "first generation up north" colored girl, the fevered storyteller, the performance addict, the woman who believed that the very first version of a poem was sacred and that nothing should ever be changed. I look at my first attempts to deal with the death of my father, and my chest fills with that hollow once again. I see all the shoes I stepped into, all the voices I tried on, all the ways I found to make my life just that much larger, and I realize that every word exists—just as it is—for the sole purpose of making me the person that I am.

So one day two decades ago, Luis Rodriguez walked up to me and said, "I'm thinking about starting a press. I'm going to publish poets I like." Then he asked if I had a manuscript and I said yes. (When someone asks you if you have a manuscript, you always say yes, whether or not you actually do.) I rushed to gather everything I had ever uttered from stage, every hurried cocktail napkin scribble, every anguished journal entry, every dimming memory.

What you hold in your hands is the breath of a young woman on the edge of everything. What you hold in your hand is my faulty, frustrating and thankful heart.

Patricia Smith
Autumn 2011

BIRTH OF THE BLUES

● Supposedly, his singing of the blues is pure recreation.
Notes wrench themselves
free over his morning coffee, ride jumbled and
 flatback
 in the immediate air.

They come sweet and choking from his long throat, flattened
third and seventh notes, way too blue for normal.

During his morning drive, he notices a window sill filled with
 dead things,
 roses, clipped violets, long forgotten, and he
 coughs a note loose. There is a fat bit of
blood clinging to it. This scares him, and he jams

his foot down on the accelerator, pressing hard through
imaginings, biting and spitting and baptizing
himself with glass. He thinks it
perhaps a momentary madness,

but a child flies twisted by the window and he knows
then he cannot stop, that he will never be able to swallow
another mouthful of grit
and cough his blues into a dead mic.

FROWNING MAN, WOOL COAT, APRIL, CHICAGO

The sun is up to its usual tricks,
slicing a sheen across flat-faced spires,
filling horrible street musicians with giddy inspiration.
Their wheezing saxophones and ill-tuned pluckings
punch holes of sour sound in new air.
How easily men are seduced by the plumpness of nickels.

Only he still smells snow. He was never
quite fooled by city sparkings, by the dusty
roll of buses into Mag Mile squares of light.

Optimists call it spring.
But the city prances its deception
each year this time,
with buildings and people still frigid at their peaks.
Why, he wonders,
are they so wary of toppling,
so anxious to believe in barely discernible sunlight,
so willing to shrug the frost from shoulders,
to tilt fleshy faces up,
to suck in mineral bursts of rain?

He pulls up the collar of his coat,
listens to the dizzy ping of street songs,
to shards of ice colliding on the lake's calm sheeting.
No one thing fools him.

He has always been able to hear despair
give way to spring with a squeak like
the breaking of rust. It happens that way
with maybe one in a million people.
The rumbling of seasons broils in the blood.

But sometimes it's summer before they hear it,
before winter surrenders and clinks into the past,
before the street musicians pick a light, poisonous melody
designed to sink violently into our winter bones.

SHIFTING BORDERS

● to escape the rain, i am drawn
into the clattering folds of the medina
where soft gold hurls brilliant. the streets simmer.
children run with dinner balanced on their shoulders.

voices click and hiss at my new tall walking:
"you pretty. pretty brown woman."
this was once a troubling revelation.

but here i am at home in my new, hard shoes.
my mouth pulls steaming chunks of mutton
from the fingers of a stranger
who then offers red silk for my hair,
musky oil for the valleys of my throat.
for a moment, his tongue wrestles with
"american?," then gives up.

as the day grows seamless, i think of my white lover,
of the ways he would try to burn this dust from my body.
we would bend at right angles against the rain,
we would hide warm, flat circles of bread beneath our clothing.

but he is an earth away, and i am taller without him.
confronted by my new geography,
even he will not remember how to touch me.
his eyes will search for the edges
he knew were once there,
his hands will move to establish new borders,
but this pretty brown woman of new tall walking
will render his fingers useless.

MEDUSA

Poseidon was easier than most.
He calls himself a god,
but he fell beneath my fingers
with more shaking than any mortal.
He wept when my robe fell from my shoulders.

I made him bend his back for me,
listened to his screams break like waves.
We defiled that temple the way it should be defiled,
squirming and bucking our way from corner to corner.
The bitch goddess probably got a real kick out of that.
I'm sure I'll be hearing from her.

She'll give me nightmares for a week or so,
that I can handle. Or she'll turn the water
in my well into blood. I'll scream when I see it,
and that will be that. Maybe my first child
will be born with the head of a fish.
I'm not even sure it was worth it,
Poseidon pounding away at me like a madman,
losing his immortal mind
because of the way my copper skin swells in moonlight.

Now my arms smoke and itch. Hard scales
are rising on my wrists like armor. C'mon Athena,
he was just another lay, and not a particularly
good one at that, even though he can spit steam
from his fingers. Won't touch him again, promise.
And we didn't mean to drop to our knees
in your temple, but our bodies
were so hot and misaligned.

It's not every day a gal gets to sample a god,
you know that. Why are you being so rough on me?
I feel my eyes twisting, the lids crusting over
and boiling, the pupils glowing like red coals.

Athena, woman to woman,
could YOU have resisted him?
Would you have been able to wait for the proper place,
the right moment, to jump those immortal bones?

Now my feet are tangled with hair, my ears are gone.
My back is curving and my lips have grown numb.
My garden boy just shattered at my feet.

Dammit, Athena, take away my father's gold. Send me away
to live with lepers. Give me a pimple or two.
But my face. To have men never again be able to gaze
at my face, growing stupid in anticipation
of that first touch, how can any woman live like that?
How will I be able to watch their warm bodies
turn to rock when their only sin was desiring me?

All they want is to see me sweat. They just want
to touch my face and run their fingers through my...

my hair

is it moving?

GOODBYE, CHARLIE

After seeing Charlie McCarthy, the late Edgar Bergen's dummy, in Chicago's Museum of Broadcast Communications.

Few of us would have believed,
but the dummy understood why he suddenly had no voice.
And although cold fists crammed their voices
into the small of his back,
although slim, probing fingers made his eyes
flap and bulge, he had no strength left
to fashion words
or to create them in the crevices of his gleaming face.

So he too wished for the perfect death
and allowed cool velvet to be draped
over still-rigid eyes,
breathing — as always — through his skin.

There was no tuxedoed straight man
in this new vertical casket,
only the ghosts of question and response.
No brittle stage lights burning into his bone,
no talking when he just didn't feel like it,
no warm, familiar hands filling the void,
becoming his blood and prompting his heartbeat.
Only this unnatural hurt called quiet.

Wouldn't be a bad life, really, this new gig.
At least he wouldn't be skipping from dingy town
to dirty city, holding his breath
in the musty box, or clicking champagne glasses
and flirting with brainless starlets.

Thank God no more blinking
against the cigar smoke in the Chez Paree,
or dressing up in that stuffy formal wear
just so foul-breathed children
could beg to feel him in their laps.
He simply didn't need them to sit upright.

With the master gone, laid down to simple silence,
Charlie knew he could still zing 'em
with the painful punchline,
but no one else could urge his lips to laughter.

Because through his eyes, moon round
and rimmed red with memory,
he swore he could plainly see his own end:

There. On the backs of his hands.
The beginnings of wood.

WITH MANY FACES

A Chicago streetwalker contemplates an unwanted pregnancy

● They always tease me about my hard hips,
about the way my wine-colored lipstick hints at
a mouth much larger than mine, about the way my raw
unnecessary singing leaves scratches in the air.
All that I can deal with —
after all, I'm the wild wind blowing through this place,
I'm the reason men wake up with mirrors on their minds.
With my plump crazy arms and hot adjectives,
I'm all the vice they need,
raging against the astonishment of a new day.
But now my belly's tight with questions and sugar words.
My blue jeans have questions.

Two hundred dollars and 20 minutes will keep me here,
cold countess of the barstool, slave to my own moisture.
Child with the voice, nose and color
        of countless chance encounters,
I have no innocence to give you.
I who respond too easily to touch,
who mothered and fathered you at the bottom of a shot glass.

But I am necessary in my own way. I don't wear my kitchen
on my back, I'm the only blue note on the jukebox,
the last chance for fuel before the freeway,
so they feel it's okay to slap me with their fat hands,
to threaten me with dull razors,
to love me until their fevers break.

Two hundred dollars and 20 minutes will find me,
pale and bloodless,
in a room of stark white and silver,
sleeping to the sound of your many sweet names
while the machine that is my body
goes about its cold business, creating scars.
I will love you as long as the soreness lasts.

Then, maybe tomorrow, I'll struggle once again in a narrow bed,
forcing myself to glow beneath some man's popeyed need,
hating the way his fingers move inside me
where my child with many faces no longer strains toward life.

ROMPER ROOM LADY

For a Romper Room
Lady who allegedly
went crazy on the
air and tried her
best to strangle
the kids.

when doorknobs began to feel cold beneath her fingers,
she dreaded the twisting,
the opening,
the biting frost and full jazz snatches
bound to slap her full in the face.

so she learned to keep her hands
very slowly at her sides
such a proper oatmeal

3.2.1. once again,
she poured her pupils tight into the camera:
i see damon. i see cara. i see michael. i see sharon.
she didn't see anyone, she never DID see anyone,
but they demanded the creation of boxtop children,
of toddlers with inquisitive blue ovals,
with As and Bs and Cs
        marching in uniform stupidity down their throats.

she sensed rebellion in the silks of their hair
she smelled something crazy
in the pale sinewy skin at their necks

she could hear their hearts beating telltale rhythm:
A, B, C, D, E, F...
NO!

if only she could pull their withery, singsong voices
away from her face,
if only her thighs didn't lean forward at night,
remembering their sputter talk,
their 60, 70 snaking fingers,
if only she didn't always brake
just short of the stoplight
(terrorized by primary colors)

never wanting to reach home
where her nights were indelibly haunted
by the farmer in the dell
and her screams were shaped
like the heads of children.

WALLS

Dedicated to the

nation's homeless.

they've become experts at the imagining of walls
molded high of odd plaster: pain. desire. deception.

they create ceilings that grow soft and heavy with
rain, or with the memory of other ceilings.

nothing reaches them. watch them now, open
non-existent closets, coughing hard at the wild
swirlings of dust. not giving a damn about the
absence of clothes there, just freaking on
the walls, the ceiling. molded of odd things:
smell. despair. sleep.

we are amazed at their bodies, which seem boneless.
curled half, bent double, the head a wall (the eyes,
however, no longer windows), the thighs a wall,
the weary back a ceiling. these sad houses
cram our doorways, are showered with sparks from
the bellies of trains, trip us on our way to work.

but door frames rattle on thin bones. we beseech
the god of walls, of ceilings. there but for
the grace of a weekly paycheck go i.
the houses unfurl in a strange, doomed dance.
no longer adept at imagining, they are
chilled by their thinness, by the bold absence
of those four deep corners,
the cracking of that odd plaster,
the bleeding of something cold from deep, deep scratches,
from holes where nails have been.
but our eyes are drawn to their dance, we who
are able to paint our walls and ceilings any
color we wish. we are drawn to their simple dance,
which is strange,
because it only seems to have two basic movements.

watch with me now, but whisper.
they do not know they are dancing.

First, arms lifted in praise of any ceiling.
Then, arms extended in the worship of walls.

KIDNAPPER

Even the candy I offer demands a smoother surface.
But a child knows rough, and wants it.
I wrap one chestnut curl around my finger
and she's all butter,
slick and boneless,
ready to pop the sugary disc into her mouth.

You just never know about kids.
I'll bet her mother told her not to talk to strangers.
But I'm beyond anything she knows.
I'm one long, cool caress, a clean curving whistle.
I beckon like jump rope.
Even my fingers sing narcotic,
circling around the bright candy wrapper
and tangling like friends in her hair.

I am her kindergarten now.
I am her soft and seamless mother,
stupid with kitchen ritual,
I am her father, who tips a final 90-proof
steam to his lips
and dreams once again of his daughter's knees
as she sucks on the mercy of bright candy.

Mother and father, I will bury your child
in sweet, unquestioning kisses,
I will lay her body down in tumbled soil,
where she will feed upon the dark.
There she will count away seconds with crayon slashes,
there she will press alphabet songs into her eyes,
there she will learn to speak to the yielding mud,
there she will learn to breathe leaves,

and oh yes,
she will wait for me

LAST NIGHT

Last night, her breasts began to swell.
"Is your body trying to tell you it
wants a baby?" he asked, too lightly,
and once again she almost felt his mouth
scripting gentle questions on her round,
moving belly, she saw the tiny child
sleeping curled and moonwashed between them,
she imagined him, bearded and bumbling,
stooped low in the supermarket checkout
with a giggling, cream-black daughter
strapped to his backside.

But this was strange country to them both,
he with four stout sons
spiraling away from regrets of their own,
she with a too-tall growler learning to curse and kiss.
By the time steam pushed them together again,
her breasts meant something else. She fell back slowly
while he cupped the left in his huge, forgiving hand.
She tensed when his knowing finger moved inside her,
where nothing strained toward living, nothing stirred.

BOY SNEEZES, HEAD EXPLODES

Inspired by a headline in a super- market tabloid

There are no pictures with this story,
strange when one considers the possibilities.

There could be a pre-sneeze montage,
dim photos of a boy being bounced
on his father's knee,
a terse 8th grade graduation shot,
or something taken at Boy Scout camp
four years ago.
Any shot with his head still
attached to his shoulders
would pretty much get the point across.

Or afterward, man-on-the-street candids
of surprised passersby
showered with bits of gray matter,
shards of nostril,
clumps of hair,
ragged shreds of facial tissue.

The tabloids could run
full color action shots
of the poor guy's torso
teetering back and forth
doing that crazy circumstance dance
and finally falling,
flopping on the sidewalk
like an orgasmic guppy.

The electronic media would be sure
to pick up the audio
as some witness jerk
mumbles "gesundheit"
or even worse,
"God bless you."

But I guess
anything in the way of illustration
would either be too early
or too late.
Who could see the pinpoint of irritation
growing insistent like a hot white light in his head?
Who could follow that errant bit of dust
driven deep by the wind?
How could he know, when he opened his mouth,
that once he closed it
it wouldn't be there?

BALANCE

For Stephen Dobyns

A young boy finds a red rubber globe on
the sidewalk. His tiny foot connects with the ball
and sends it soaring, but it plops down
and settles rather violently in his upturned eye.
The eye waters and swells, the boy screams.

A man walking by remembers a similiar predicament
from his youth, and smiles. He tries to tell
the boy his story, but the lad is not to be
consoled. The ball meanwhile has rolled away to
find another niche in the tall, wind-shivered grass.

The man leaves the boy sitting on the curb, crumpled
and brooding and bitter. Later that evening, while
his wife and children devise new ways to avoid him,
the man suddenly realizes there is a certain beauty
in balance. He sits at the dinner table with one eye closed,

notes the altered perspective,
and dutifully points his working eye in the direction
of his wife's open mouth. Then he takes a deep
breath and shuts the other eye. He nibbles at his
dinner that way, delighted at the discovery

that his surroundings are conquered so easily.
He thinks of the boy. Before slamming a swift
door shut on the memory, he idly wishes he'd
had the compassion and presence of mind
to sock the little bastard in his other eye.

MARCH 19, 1890

*Only once has
Mississippi executed
a white man in the
death of a Negro.
On March 19, 1890,
M.J. Cheatham of
Tennessee was
hanged in Grenada,
Miss. for shooting
James Tillman in
the back and dump-
ing his body in the
Yalobusha River.*

the grass hisses in grenada, mississippi. full of
a rollicking life, an affirmation of cycles. noon
rolls in on heat. crooked buildings sigh dust.
fat flies hover and conspire to annoy. but his
head denies their presence. he bows low against
scissors of sun and decides against needing the
cool wind that must be blowing somewhere, far away
from this keen, slamming smell, these hot midday ribbons.

his mood is almost jovial. dammit if life don't
twist strange sometimes, he thinks, and a dry
chuckle erupts, startling the men who eye him
with poison in mind. they are waiting to
cradle his head, to search in vain for his heartbeat,
to pester his ashen skin with sour breathing.

let them wait. someone passes whiskey, designed
to fuel his climb up a hill crooked and rustling
with dark buzzing, to speed his lazy approach to
the circle of hemp. the hot liquid cramps his
tongue, explodes in the cavities at the back of his
mouth. ain't this just to end all, he whispers, ain't
this just the final straw, the bad turn, the dream
you never wake up from. just one nigger gone,

not like the slapping of a woman or the murdering
of something human. it's almost to laugh, ain't
it, ain't it, but something disagrees in the
climbing. no final, ragged holes for him, edged
in sudden blood. no turned back, no blessed
ignorance, no muddied river to cushion the
fall, no uncertain bottom to bounce upon,

only the heat and the low whizzing of plump flies.
only something wild and unbelieving inside, a whisper
and then a scream for wind. any wind. but even
upon wind, his final question won't be heard.

SCREAM

For Michael Brown

A friend noticed it first:
the way I would carefully place my left hand
in the hollow at the center of my chest
and work while it rested there, as if
establishing a silent communion
with whatever pulsed within.

If only she could have felt you there, screaming.

This turmoil frightens me. I'm sure everyone
can see it. I'm certain that my eyes have
grown large, that I babble on in thin,
nonsensical threads. I have seen my feet tangle.
Only when I sit very still and feel

the seed you've left pounding inside me,
do I grow awed at the stupidity of rhythm.
My only sense is the sense of your mouth
everywhere on me. The rhymes you crafted this
morning won't stop singing on my skin.

"He looks a little like Santa," I'll tell my
friend, just to make her laugh. But I do not
move my hand, or speak to her of the gifts
you bring. I can only drown in the sound
no one else seems to hear, that steady work
from the niche you've carved at my chest,
that scream, that inexplicable scream,
that sound of one man patiently prying
at the fingers of this fist I call my heart.

BOWLING AT MARIGOLD LANES
AT 4:13 AM

I am in line for shoes, just behind the man
who splits his paycheck with Jesus.
Our various facts, fictions and fevers
have slapped us from sleep,
and Lord, we have come to bowl.

A woman, her hair exploding in pink foam rollers,
tells a friend how Negroes used to have to step off the curb
into the street when a white person was walking toward them.

She is walking toward me as she says this.

While I am not looking,
she thinks about spitting into my Pepsi,
pulls out a pearlized custom ball,
and heads for lane number three.
There, I assume, she intends to bowl.

The man who peddles women's bodies for a living
is disgusted when he finds their smell still on
his fingers. So he jams those red digits
deep into the recesses of a Brunswick,
imagines silken hairs on the pins,
and begins to bowl.

The 86 average in the third lane from the door
still refuses to believe that Rock Hudson
walked both sides of the fence. She wears a vial
of Elvis' sweat like a talisman between parched breasts,
slides her size nines toward the middle arrow,
and my God, she bowls.

Stuffing regret down the waist of our Sansabelt slacks,
we bowl.
With children at home waiting for their dinners,
we bowl.
With acned ears, we listen to the sweet talk of a man
who picks rumors from his nose. We lust after the queens
of freeze-dried housewares, and we bowl, we bowl.

Then there are the pretenders,
the aerobicizers with detachable blue collars. Like me,
wasting my footsteps on the bell of 4:13 a.m.,
sniffing hard rows of blue, black and pearl,
just looking for a ball I like.

NO GAS

After seeing a poster
offering a $10,000
reward for the
murderer of a
female gas station
attendant in the sad
little town of
Carlin, Nevada.

You can stop honking that damned horn.
I don't pump no gas,
I don't wipe no windows or check no oil.
I'm not here to fuel your dreams.
I'm paid to take your money.

I'll play the smalltown promise
if that's what you need to get your ass in gear,
but I won't let you breathe with me.
I won't let you touch me
any longer than you need to
while you're passing along that sweaty dollar.

I coulda been a hairdresser. Right up the street,
they just opened up one of them beauty shops
with those chairs that move the way
they need your head to move. I don't have to be here.
I graduated 8th grade with no problem.
I could take my long legs to Vegas, make real money.

Just pay for your gas. Go back to your car, go back
to your fat wife who's snoozing her way through Nevada.
I got no flashes of skin for you here.
        And stop telling me to smile.

It took three days to scrub her blood off the shelves,
sticky and scarlet and crammed between the cash register keys
and the poster don't tell you I'm the one who found her,
6 a.m., her body laid open like a question that keeps asking,
her mouth fixed in that dead circle and me slipping on the
bubbles coming out of her. Always talking bout
how this town was too small, how some sharp talker
from the East was sure to notice her heart on her sleeve.

He sure did notice it. Left it on the counter with his change.
Left it there for me to find.

Two years of days are gone now, poster big on the wall
like some twisted joke, Janet hanging over my head
smiling like she didn't breathe her last that night,
like the smell of her screaming ain't still here.
She learned to take the money,
but she never learned to let go of the hand.

I coulda been a hairdresser. Don't have to be here.
Count your change, but hurry it up, get back on the road.
And tell that guy behind you to lay off the damned horn.

I don't pump no gas.
Don't wipe no windows.

LAKE MICHIGAN
AT SHERIDAN ROAD, 2/8/87

● you batter ugly earth bruise
you ice drip trees you brutal
thunder kiss
you white foam crashes and slow rape
you slap fast and leave scars
you jump break and eat wall
you swirl deep and spit high

you wash blue ink from night
you cause us terror eyes
you round roll and spurt
you suck sound from street
you eat pieces of street
you pull lazily at branch and root

you cold slick silver glaze
you wave swallow hope
of morning calm. were you
always a sheet of smooth above, were
you always boiling beneath?

REVELATION AT MOODY'S PUB

........................●we seem to have done untold harm to romance,

I discuss love with a   just the two of us, you with your bitter dances

cynical friend.   to the rhythms of rum, me holding myself too tightly.

i need you the way i have you now, your bravado
peeled back to reveal poems, your hands motionless
on the table, that graying wisp of hair
refusing to stay tucked behind your ear.

i needed to see what i did,
you dizzy with the terms of seduction,
dragging your fingers along a willing thigh,
exploring her throat with your own,
forgetting to meet my eyes across the room.
i need to feel you wanting to

slam your glass down, i need you to say it,
i don't believe in love. go on, say it, i don't
believe in love, until you convince me that i
don't believe in it either and we sit bleak
and emptied over steaming drinks. ache
me

with your hollow words, poet. shame me
with those lines about that perfect world
we no longer believe in

where you tease the backs of my knees with flowers
and i touch your glistening scars with my mouth.

FIRE

Last night, a Wicker Park two-flat burned to the ground.
I watched the fire for what seemed like hours,
ashamed of my obsession with the edges of temperature,
shamelessly craving the dark oily smell,
the sad curl of furniture, the mad slapping sound.

It burned the way the boys on my street burn,
the ripe, brown, seamless boys of Paulina,
beautiful and idle beneath the sun's copper push.
I once believed they were the source of my fever.

I am suspicious of their hissing, their motives,
but I am full of their black razored hair, their eyes like stormwater,
and their muscled forearms braced just outside the open
windows of cars. I want to scream the short city blocks
in their low riders, the bass line bringing pain to my mouth,
whipping across this tuneless city
like a match across the face of a matchbook.
I want to feel the road burn beneath us.
I want to feel their stomach muscles
move like snakes
beneath the pads of my restless fingers.

Last night, a woman in Wicker Park lost her baby to the fire.

I locked my eyes on the flames like a brainless child,
like a hungry woman with heat my only language,
while the woman's screams wrote a bitter poem on the hot air
and lean shirtless boys belched Budweiser toward the flames.
Acceptance, they realized, is the only true solution.
It is a lesson the grieving mother will learn soon.

I watched the fire for hours. It burned the way I burn
when you slip a thick finger into me, when my voice
breaks in my throat and my body pours hallelujahs
into the cup of your hand. Watching the flames,
I wanted my hair to hurt with smoke. When your
body covered mine that night, I wanted to be blacker,
to be unbearably hot, to hiss when you touched me.
I wanted my new skin to crackle beneath you.
I wanted your mouth to become a huge, impossible circle
as you began to burn, screaming that mother's first scream.

YOUR MAN

Your man walks in on wishbone legs,
smelling like hot sauce and black pepper,
bringing me blues bound up like roses
every Thursday night 'bout this time.

Your man brings me sweet bread and fried corn,
feeds me like an animal from his fingers,
tames me like an animal with his hips.
Your man comes in sweatin' his blue collar
and singin' those lies, those washaway dreams.

I wait for his mouth, the mercy circle.
I wait for his mouth. The mercy circle.
He neatly arranges the gasping of my skin,
leaves me gentle and crazed on a trembling bed.

Your man's lovin' leaves marks like drumbeats,
disturbances on brown skin stretched across a circle of bone.
I carved his coming out of a mojo moonlight,
out of what you told me
about the voodoo in his fingers.

He says "Bitch, lie still," and I do. I do.
He says "Squeeze harder," and I want to.
Your man hurls light against my skin
and forgets your name when that's what I need.

Yeah. Your man is your man,
but he visits me sometimes,
he rocks the house sometimes,
he shakes it up sometimes,
he makes it right. All the time.
Sometimes.

PRETENDING THE GHOST

I was raised in the
Baptist church.
Every Sunday, my
mother would "get
the spirit." Since the
same thing wasn't
happening to me,
I thought something
was wrong. So one
Sunday, I pretended.

● Every Sunday morning,
I wondered what it was
that made my mother
rumble.

Was it the Rev. Matthew Thomas,
72 years of spirit in his spine
propelling him across the pulpit
like hot air popcorn?
Was it the way his bended body
stiffened with the message,
God's wagging finger
swelling his throat with howling,
or the veins in his head bulging in time
with the choir's doo wop rhythm?

Was it the gut songs of the devout,
who truly, truly believed,
women with hats like satin ski slopes
and men with Saturday night's whiskey
still steaming from their pores?

I'd sit there, perfect in pink anklets and pigtails,
praying to the 3-D cardboard Christ
to please not let my mother embarrass me.
But sure enough,
when the Rev spit the right wail in her direction
(accompanied by a hop, skip and jump
his body was clearly incapable of),
I saw my mother's toes curl.

Her eyes would roll back into her head,
her face would twist,
and I couldn't help thinking
that she looked constipated instead of possessed.
Someone would whisk me away,
and when I came back

her stockings would be down around her ankles,
her eyeglasses would be cracked,
and for the rest of the service
she'd be rocking like the Temptations
and whispering in some alien tongue.
My mother no more, my mother still.

Later she'd say, "Just the spirit got in me, chile,
that's all."
Couldn't figure out why the spirit wasn't gettin' in me too.

So two weeks later,
I kicked,
screamed,
slapped two deacons,
showed by best underwear to the congregation,
lost my favorite hair ribbons,
three buttons
and a front tooth.

My mother wept, clearly overwhelmed
at my performance
and God's entrance into my 6-year-old soul.
God, however,
gazing at me from a blacklight version
of the Last Supper,
clearly could not take a joke.

It was at that moment he condemned me to a life
of sloppy kisses from men with post-nasal drip,
a life ruled by the fake father,
the pseudo son,
and the phony ghost.

WALLENDA

Our most memorable days are marked by an absence of control.

Suppose he woke that morning, showered, shaved
and pulled a brush through his thinning hair.
Suppose breakfast served no practical purpose.
Suppose he wondered for hours what shoes to wear,
as if it would make a difference.
Suppose he began thinking about the inevitability of floors.
Suppose his blood grew thick with warning
and his feet refused to follow one after the other.
Suppose his body stuttered with denial.
Suppose this time he looked up at it,
the wire that curved all wrong in the wind, and
suppose a scream rumbled behind his lips like a runaway train.
Suppose the climb up was as unnecessary as the climb down.
Suppose fear was a fever kinking his hair.
Suppose the last word on his hands was flying.

Do *you* find walking a little difficult lately?
Have the toes of your shoes begun to curl away from the wire?
Like the cat waking on the ledge after a crazed sleep,
do you take that first resolute step into nothing

and wait for the air to control you?

NAWLINS TANGO

For Tony

Fitzpatrick

● be inspired
by the beckoning wail of the whitest rum.
be moved
by the whispery clink of papercup crystal.
don't wait for the music to say something nasty.
why break your stride? come on in.

slam your arms and legs against the unquestioning dark.
do it like it should be done,
tilt your pelvis toward the bass player.
count the seconds
until blood begins to pop from the tips of his fingers,
already tangled and swollen in their chaos of string.

let layers of solemn smoke settle on your hair.
stop breathing daylight. forget the world
that shudders outside, with its violent profusion
of flowers, its concrete boxes,
its improper pulsing.

find what you've been wanting right here.
spit tequila into someone's eyes.
succumb to the mad press of music.
it's the bass player's fault, all the bass player's fault.
he's found the booming in you
and made it the booming in him.

so the hell with what your mama told you,
dance in the worst way.
dance upside down,
on your hair, on your knees,
dance tight and illegal,
dance on the rule book, sister,
dance on the flag, brother,
dance until your legs lock,
until the lights scream on
and sunday morning
leaves a message for you at the door.

dance until the bastard sun finds you
crumpled on the sidewalk outside,
your shoes torn into neat republican pieces
and flecks of the bass player's blood
glowing like a come-on in your hair.

THE POETRY WIDOW

You've known me long enough to know
that my longings are sometimes without reason.

Tonight, I wished I was one of your poems,
strong syllables curled in your throat
awaiting a joyous delivery. I wished I
was that clever, stilted script on the
paper in your hand, words you sweat over.

I wanted to feel your thick hands move over me,
urging my spirit from the page. Tonight, as I
crawled into old music and warm, scented water,
as I filled myself with the steamed onions and rice
you'd left for me, as I wondered aloud about the hole
in the middle of the room where I stood,

I wished I was one of your poems. I wanted to be
a strong movement in your mouth, a shock to your audience.
I wanted your first and last word to be me. I needed applause.

JUKEBOX

Hey mister, that's me up on the jukebox
I'm the one who's singing this sad song
Well, I'll cry everytime you slip in one more dime
And let the boy sing the sad one one more time.

— *James Taylor*

●longer than i care to admit
i been slinging the brew in this place
filling 'em up and pushing 'em across
etching grooves in the grease on the bar
and wearing the night
like it's got my name on it

there's just one thing gets to me
night after night,
it's the way they walk in, and right away
they ask for change
beating a path to the dream box
and peeling back their pain in 4/4 time

i watch the damn thing suck in their silver
and feed them back the beating of their own hearts
disguised as drumbeats
or that rebel guitar lick
or that first slow moan in K-19:

i did you wrong
my heart went out to play
but in the game i lost you
what a price to...

you know, it just beats my skin thin
that soft, stupid plop the disc makes when it drops
and the way the crazy dreamers just stand there
their hopeful eyes locked on the lights
while the box shouts out their hurting
for everyone to hear
and for a few cruel people
to dance to

like her. watching her walk in, smooth,
like she's balancing on that last beam of moon,
i mix her first drink in my head
she'll want something with edges,
something deep and poisonous,
a memory hot at the back of her throat.

and i'll pour it for her,
turning my eyes away,
imagining her unsure ankles
wrapped tight around the barstool's bottom

and oh yeah
she swivels toward me and she's fever
the air around her wet with wanting
and i'm drawn in, goddamn stupid barkeep,
just like i always am

and just as i'm calling back my heartstrings
just as her eyes are saying
dream baby, baby dream on me,
just as her words begin rubbing hard
at the small of my back,
just like clockwork

she asks for change

and as she walks to the dream box
there are tears in the bend of her back

hey mister
(she asks for change)
that's me
(and walks like moon beaming)
up on the jukebox
(the dimes like steam in her fist)
i'm the one
(she punches one letter, one number)
who's singing this sad song
(the platter falls flat. and crisp.)
well i'll cry everytime
(just like clockwork)
you slip in one more dime
(peeling back her pain)
and let the boy sing the sad one
(in 4/4 time)
one more time
(in 4/4 time)
one more time
(just like)
one more time
(clockwork)

MY FRIEND PREPARING
FOR THE END OF LOVE

My friend is busy packing away mental provisions,
snuggling into a corner of his Clark St. bunker,
waiting for the thunder that ends romance.
He wakes up each morning in a body that's new to him,
one that's limp and weary with want,
one that's battered by need.
Often, she's there. Her heat is the poem
he can't write, her smile a rhyme trapped in his pen.

But she doesn't seem to require poems,
and that confuses him. He needs to have her
neatly squared upon a page, all rhythm and nuance,
tucked safely ahead of those words "The End."
Failing that, he listens carefully for silence
in her eyes, for regret in her walk. He listens
until he is dim and crazy with waiting,
like a fear-frozen animal in the path of a car.

It is pain to see him building, blindly
weaving a safe place from her hair, her sweat.
The bunker grows high and bends, heavy with the
weight of pulses pounding, with kisses that twist
surprised mouths. Sighing, she touches his wet skin.
He breathes in, sensing the imminent fall
of the curtain, his heart carefully balanced
on the very, very edge of a shelf of clouds.

MARIA

"Do you need help?"
"My name is Maria."
"Are you cold? Are you hungry?"
"My name is Maria."

Maria wakes up and screams with her shoulders
but another sun passes
and another moon passes
before she pulls back the skin
that stretches across her eyes
and converses with the concrete in whispers.

Yesterday she sat tall and straight
in a hard metal chair, her toes
all crazy nervous drumming, her head
feeling pinched and steamy
beneath flourescent lights,
and listened as the helpless helped her
to help herself
by saying, "We can't help you."

She remembers her elbows growing red
against the thin rough threads of a borrowed jacket.
She remembers thinking, "But I can type."

She must have felt bare and cheapened
beneath the lights, because this morning she woke up
on the ground right outside good times,
breathing walls
and talking for hours with her bone,
calling for help with her shoulders.

But she stands up anyway. She gets right up.
She's Maria. Her belly was once broad with children.
If you touched her hair with your tongue,
the bitterness would drive you back and down.

She's Maria. She opens her thighs
and lets in slivers of sun. She's Maria,
the woman of six syllables.

Born into a hell of bricks, now without a home,
without songs, without beams of moon, without
qualifications, without words, without help,
without a warm coat, with tender touching.
Tonight she knows only snow will cushion her sleep.
But she stands up. She gets right up. And she walks.
Because even though that cold metal chair
carved its message into the small of her back,

her name's still Maria. She's brown and strong.
She can type, dammit. Her shoulders say so.

BUCKET OF BLOOD

An infamous rib joint, the Bucket of Blood, is a violent, yet well-patronized spot in Chicago's South Lawndale ghetto. Lately it's become fashionable for Yuppies, giddy after a night in the Lincoln Ave. blues bars, to visit the Bucket for a latenight snack.

You order the hot links because you like them,
not because the man breathing hard beside you,
the one who smells like he could kill you
with one well-timed punch, wants you to order them.
He doesn't say a word, or even look at you,
but you know to order them with hot pepper, extra sauce.
Then you're a Saturday night rebel,
a Chi-Town freedom fighter,
you're the 2 a.m. white boy at the Checkerboard Lounge,
you're nobody's fool,
and there's no reason you can't stride into south Lawndale
and order up some hot links.

But baby, this ain't quasi anything,
this is the Twilight Zone that killed Rod Serling,
this is the Bucket of Blood.
Men, crazy in their quest for pork,
have died approaching its doors.
And that's Cool Breeze standing next to you.
There ain't no words for his kind of ugly.

Breeze has been knifed so many times
the left side of his face just seems to be crawling.
The bone beneath has given up.
But you'd better not stare,
just bite into your links,
let the juice snake down your arms,
and keep your eyes straight ahead.
You'd better not lock your eyes in on his face,
that startled map of bad moves and wrong choices.

You see, Breeze is a blues man, but he's big,
and when you're living the way he does,
knowing how to shake the mic is not enough,
knowing how to crawl up the ladies skirts
with a done-me-wrong won't get him over,
he's got to be the baddest ass,
got to run something,
and the Bucket of Blood is turf enough.

Old grease makes the walls slick,
pepper and smoke eat at your eyes,
and once in a while, the odd white boy walks in,
drunk on Lite beer, American history and good intentions.
Breeze don't say nothing.
He just stays blue-black, the left side of his face
bopping to some rhythm you can't pin down,
something that hasn't popped up in sociology class just yet.
Yeah, Breeze is a blues man, a crazy riff with no end note,
and you think you can help mold the music, but go on, go on,
order some more hot links, hot peppers, extra sauce.
Ignore the old man with cheap whiskey beating him down,
don't study the wound or ask the question,
'cause right now you're just north side enough
to be west side for two hours a week.

Just stand there until he comes to you,
chuckling low and gritty in his throat
and smiling like a stringless guitar.
Just wait until his face melts in your direction,
until he shouts out what your hungry heart has come to hear:
"You crazy coming out here, white boy?
Get your ass over here and sit down.
And bring those links with you."

THE AWAKENING

*The assignment —
write a poem about
trees for Chicago's
"Poem for Osaka"
contest. The prize —
a trip to Osaka,
Japan, as our city's
cultural ambassa-
dor. This poem,
written from the
point of view of a
tree on Chicago's
lakefront, won top
honors.*

● Since mother morning wiped clean
the chaotic slate of starlight,
hard winds have forced the tree to beg.
She bends and splinters, bracing against
their steady push, her spindly brown fingers
cramped in stretch toward an impossible solace.
All of her strains toward the sun, which is
now just a pulse in the lightening sky without
the strength to poke its teasing slivers of light
through the solid gray cloak of clouds.
To move minutes, she curls her toes deep into
moist ribbons of soil. Her skin grows wet.
The lake roars in, chilling her thick ankle,
and she whistles her sudden ache toward
the skyline, with its bright confusion of
buildings and sound. The sun chuckles low in his
throat, watching her fingers freeze and crack.
Suddenly he smacks one of her glistening sides
with heat. She rises on her toes and once again
throws her tired, cold body open to her bold,
regretless love, while the lake curls away and
the wind dies to a whisper: "Tomorrow."
The tree stands taller, begins to breathe in
voices, rhythms, the blessing of sun.
She knows many things, much more than the
body suddenly flat against her, seeking shade.
She knows the lovers who stop to scratch
their hopeful names into her skin.
She knows the uncertain geography of rainfall.
And she has a name for the moan that worries gently in her hair.
It is called Chicago.

THE RIVER

We arrived at the river too late. Even the trees smelled dark,
dappled with the memory of departed light, all semblance
    of music squeezed from their battered bark.
We had hoped to find the river singing.
Instead we found you, bound my moving mud, your body
broken bone by black bone, and laid there to rest.

They said the speckled water was used to moments like you.
There was just no way to doubt that. Pieces of screams floated to
the bleak surface and brushed against our astonished ankles.
We worked in silence. There was some bad joking, but I was the
only one who noticed when stars began to bulge from the socket
where your eye had been.

I used to wonder what it would be like to be born colored.
One summer the sun beat my back red and I knew,
    or thought I knew,
because the heat made my head feel small and useless.
Later when I told my wife she squeezed her eyes shut until tears
popped through her closed lids. She laughed just that hard.
That night at the river, when I pulled at your arm, the skin
came off right in my hand. I pulled just that hard.

Nights are kinda quiet out here, and this one was no different.
We peeled you away from that mud, not to save your soul, but
just so the river would sing again. We freed the living things
caught in your hair, the fish hooks that sparkled silver in your skin.
I held my breath and wanted it to be over. I wanted to go home,
to kiss my sleeping wife, to smell the sour curve behind her ear.

Nights are kinda quiet out there, and this one was no different.
None of them are different now.
    I turn on my tired shoulder to sleep
and your muddy face rises inside my head, the way it was when we
first found it, your one eye spilling stars, your mouth a horrible O,
no sound coming out, but drowning out the river's song anyway.

THE PULL

For Michael, who I
tried to push away

Like an animal intrigued by the trap,
my self, my silly bones,
arch toward you,
begging to be examined, then snapped.
I hook my hands under the rough
wooden rim of my seat to hold my body down.
I cling so desperately, and for so long,
my fingers take splinters and bleed.
Everything quakes before your cool green eyes.

Even weather seems to slide across the world toward you.
Voices sizzle low like overdue rain, but all I hear
is the wet hiss of bodies meeting, slapping, sliding.
I drink too much.
I'm calmed by daddy tequila,
keeping the glass tilted to my lips
to keep my lips on the glass
to keep my lips away from you.
All of you beckons, and I sweat it, leaning in,
wanting my clothes to be gone,
wanting your teeth to nip at the edges of this heat,
needing to feel your warm flat hands
move against all this yearning.

I bolt from the table and run away again, but my
ass quivers crazily, the skin just beneath my skirt rumbles,
and I begin a fractured moonwalk back in your direction.
I clamp onto the edge of the bar, my feet
flying out behind me. Glasses and bottles swirl in the air.
The power of the pull knocks crazy verbs
from the mouths of poets. We're all lost in it.
I run toward you again.

To get away, I lift my skirt up to my chin
and climb the jukebox with brown, bare legs,
my escape powered by steam, the drag from my
fingers pulling paper from the walls. I move
across the junky ceiling, swinging bulb to bulb,
both toward and away from the sex in your teeth,
toward and away from your mouth and fingers,
toward and away from the yin and the yang.

My nipples harden even though your lips are
across the room, and suddenly it's summer in hell.
My hands move to rub my throat, my breasts, my feet,
the confused skin inside my thighs.

I seek refuge in a musky corner,
gulping in the smell of old sorrows, breathing animal.
My body won't stop jerking, toward you,
toward the glisten of dirty midnights,
toward you, you beckoning with a hunter's know-how,
pulling, hissing, weakening my resolve,
drawing me closer, tighter, closer, tighter, then I'm running,
running, running until my feet twist, running until my chest
    shakes,
running until I see you running toward me,
your weapon leveled,
your aim undeniably true.

I pull back my lips to bare my teeth.
And then I leap.

DYING WOMAN GIVES BIRTH

Dedicated to Anna

Holmes, 4/28/88.

A friend, Anna,

walked into a video

store with her three

children as it was

being robbed. Before

the robbers left, they

shot her while her

children watched.

Anna was eight

months pregnant.

She gave birth to her

son as she was dying.

The infant was in critical condition Saturday,
weakened by erratic blood rhythms,
by detached, smooth voices that sought to feed him fever.
In his tenth moment, he ached at the falling of floors.
In his tenth year, he will slake his thirst in a river of walls.

Tubes were used to construct the child. As a man,
he will be mornings of cold coffee and impossible angles.
He will pose uncomfortable questions concerning sunrise,
yet no one will bother to chronicle his struggles against music.
There will be much frantic dancing to avoid the scream.

Condition guarded. He will grow facial hair, make love
to warm, defeated women, define his edges as the rims
of empty shot glasses, in pointless blocks of prose.
And he will sense blood in the simplest things.
Wildflowers. Clothing. Wood.

Should he live, at 30 years his bones will grow thin.
Even rain will hurt. Each sixtieth second
will roar upon him with a sudden clamping of air,
a denial of food, a silencing of breast music.
He will often relive the spilling out.

And the years will go on that way,
with a photograph of your face hot and foreign in his hand,
but no pictures of the two of you together.
His lips will touch it, again, again,
and time will pass in that futile kiss,
with his ears straining,
waiting to translate as memory scribbles its furious song:
Anna.
Anna.

BREAKHEART

For artificial heart recepient William Schroeder, who knew.

were you ever able to stop listening for it,
your ear odd-angled at your chest?
it was a tenuous rhythm, all crossed
fingers on the downbeat,
and your eyes, mood and soul
were riveted to its blood tickings.
after all, if a man could design it,
a woman could break it.
it was, by all accounts, fallible
and could be crushed like the faces of dolls.

despite its discreet and cryptic cadence,
its bop beat, its cold and maddening efficiency,
you wished it end, the mad metronome pulsing
of the made thing, so unlike those plump
kindergarten cutouts with arrows slicing their
middles. the damn plastic fist simply refused
to skip at the memory of lost-ago lovers,
there was just no clean slate
for the scribbling of desire.

so, in the end
there was just your neck twisted and aching,
and your ear straining to hear
the fluid whoosh
of life being processed.
too weary, too thin,
frightened of sleep, it was you
who doomed the blood to its stillness.

during dim and wistful hours, it was you
who patiently designed the scars needed to
seal the throbbing place, leaving us
to find reassurance in the hail of headlines:
the old ticker didn't stop, his body just got tired,
broken by less predictable things — too many midnights
in the sad shape of questions, too much soft food,
too much garish white, too much goddamn beeping.

your body just shut down,
a mere shell around the made thing,
which was still precise,
impervious,
in place.

HEADBONE

A 35-year-old
"pillar of the
community" was
charged with the
rape and murder
of his 4-year-old
daughter.

You could almost say it was her fault.
Last night, she pushed her fingertips
deep into the kinks of her hair. "Look, Daddy.
I can feel my head bone."
Then she asked him to feel her head bone too,
and he did, pressing tender with his fat, clumsy fingers,
pressing until she laughed like the dropping of flowers,
pressing until something raw welled up inside,
until he could almost feel the soft bone
move like milk beneath his hands.

When his need moved to her shoulders,
he locked in on their smooth slope
and her blouse slammed to the floor
like a door he couldn't go through again.
It's a new game, he told her, not lying exactly,
undressing her slowly
by the lazy light of the network news,
making up the rules as he went along.
His baby had always loved games.

Dammit, it was all her,
sweet and solid and willing,
her eyes dizzy with a trust that filled him full.
It was all him,
tired of running the tightrope,
needing this tiny, precise answer,
not needing to remember the question.
So he pressed himself through her,
into her,
and imagined a no-sound
like a cloud ripping apart before a storm.
The moving was sugar.
Then fire.
Then sugar.
Then fire.
She was sugar with her edges on fire.

Afterwards, she just wasn't right anymore.
She was a new and noisy thing,
her skin gone crazy beneath him,
spitting and kicking his thighs blue
with jump rope legs. And suddenly she was just
another Madison St. whore
snarling at his English and his underwear.
Anyone could see you could almost say it was her fault.

All four years of her
plotting to drag him down in this,
his finest hour.
He was mean. She was gonna tell mommy.
She didn't love him anymore.

So it was true. Love was something you bargained for.
He'd win this time.
As her screams moved from room to room in his head,
he found her skull and held on,
pressing until he heard the headbones ticking,
pressing until they caved in softly like a domino house,
pressing until she stopped rising to slap him,
pressing until she was his angel again.
Silent. Open. And ready to play a new game.

And he waited.
"I know! Let's stay up late and look at comic books."
He waited.
"Y'know sweetheart, I bet there's something good on TV."
He waited.
"Look honey, I've got a headbone too," and he stood
in the dark like an idiot,
probing his thinning hair with frantic fingers
and laughing a hurting laugh
that brought him to his knees.

And that's how they found him,
crouched over his greatest sin,
staring at the bright, slick statements
she'd left on his fingers
and waiting for the one word
that would make it all right again:

"Daddy?"

COHERENT LIGHTWAVES

● threads of brilliance from the tip of my finger
to the curve of the silly throb you've named heart,
they are their own suns, their own moons,
these beams that spit thoughtless, like first kisses.
the most economical of lovers, we have banished
verbs, choosing instead to converse skin to skin.
in this way, we flirt daily with explosion.

talk to me.
our touchwords beat together in pockets of their own syntax,
they are portents of trembling,
they are luminous beads that journey mapless from soul to soul,
they slap together our thoughts, our hips,
    our unthinking mouths,
they are lightwaves that pull me to you.

FIREWORKS

He should have known long ago how crazy
it would become. His young fingers would
chatter and ache as he crammed the gunpowder
into the hollow paper tubes, bending over his
cluttered desk in the dark. He'd cough and
wheeze and itch as the powder left its stink
scars on the back of his hands and poked at
his eyes. Then he'd slam the screen door on
the way out with his precious cargo, lie
with his back glued to the earth, and he'd let
them fly. Jesus, how his body would quake, how
the colors would break through his hands and slap
his name on the still blue blanket. Then he'd sleep
there, with the hard smell closing his face and
his father yelling "stupid nerd kid" from
the upstairs window. He should have known then
how crazy it would become, how people would
begin to ask if he dreams in color or black
and white, how he'd have to say he never
dreams because he never sleeps. He still spends
midnights with his body breaking the mud,
watching the greens spurt, pivot and pop,
watching the reds and blues link in glorious
circles. He knows he should stop, that he should
go inside where his woman lies waiting like a
spoon for him, where he'd fit neat and colorless
like the gloss of moon in her hair. But love
just wastes his time. He wants to be outside on
his knees in the damp grass, looking up.
He wants to swallow his tears and blame them on fire.
He wants to make screams in the sky.

For Michael Clark

MAYDAY

A secret fearful flier, I was fascinated to learn that Al Haynes landed Flight 232 in Sioux City with a completely powerless airplane.

All day, he'd been whipping boy for the little tragedies —
a missed breakfast,
a button popping like mystery from his cuff,
his wife narrowing her tired eyes and whispering,
"We have to talk."

He'd ridden even that familiar wave with a straightened spine,
thinking of blue, always thinking of blue,
the cold, airless blue of height,
the blues of tolerated women,
the blues of feet pressing against ground.

But now the shell freezes beneath him,
dies around his scrambling fingers
and falls like a bird wearing too many bullets.
He rides on the back of nothing.

And he begins to scream hold on, hold on,
hold on to the useless splinters of morning,
hold on to a woman's hair,
hold on to whatever says let go,
but the roar of failure just grows flat and loud.
Men swear they never wail and pray this way.

The throat of the bird quivers and cracks, cracks again.
The air rock, the ground shifting, he blinks against steam
and holds on, holds on,
and when the blue stops he is holding on to nothing
and there is nothing behind him.
Nothing.
He is rocking on his head
and the tips of his fingers are on fire.

But even that doesn't matter, as long as he can
keep his eyes away from the ground above him,
which is not blue,
which is suddenly speckled dark and wet with losing.

His eyes lock on the space
where the missing button should be.
It takes him an hour to scream.

A SHAPE HE NEEDED

● Now that I remember
Now that I can think clearly
without his fingers to distract me,
he never did sleep the night through,
not the whole time we was married.
His breath would always catch on the
broken edge of dreaming, he'd dress me
in some other woman's name,
and I'd beat his fevers away
with the flat, cool part of my arms.

Sometimes it would be days
before my face became a shape he needed.

Just a man's way, I'd say,
a small price to pay for a roof over my head,
four walls, and a belly always tight
with his black-haired children.
He was breathing the blood then,
but I couldn't see it.
I didn't know that every night in my bed
was a thin scream,
that when he pulled me into the shaking circle
of his arms, it was only my pulse that mattered.

When we fought, like women and men were meant
to do, he'd swallow his anger whole.
It throbbed like a restless stone in his neck
and he'd take me then,
white hot and mindless,
a wet, flat smacking from behind,
that sound only a wife believes.

*An episode of
"America's Most
Wanted" told the
tale of a man,
living a quiet
suburban life with
his wife and kids,
who was wanted for
murdering the
members of his pre-
vious family. Here's
his second wife, after
discovering that her
husband is not the
man she thinks he is.*

Did I tell you how much time would pass
before my face became a shape he needed?
Or that he never did sleep the night through,
not the whole time we was married?

Propped up on pillows, he'd drink warm tap water
from my cupped hands, pulling my fingers one by one
into his mouth. And now all I can remember
is the two of us trying to find sleep again,
his trigger finger barely brushing my ear, my throat,
and his lips forcing my legs apart
like bullets on their way home.

SLOW DANCE

All night long, he be watchin' me dancing,
wit his old sef, didn't need to be there anyhow
sucking on that hard liquor, all in everybody's way,
with his gray hair pushed all 'round on his head,
trying to look young. Wouldn't know house music
if it was in his own house. Rockin' his body
all off the beat, just bout falling off the barstool.
Why don't he just go hang out at that place
over on Roosevelt with the rest of them dried up folks
steada here staring at something he don't know nothing bout?

I just keep on dancing like he wasn't even there.
I learned my body early. I can make it
crawl into the music and work from the inside out.
I was built wide and mellow for the slow,
I'm boneless to find the drumbeat.
My tango is technotronic.

He walk away to pee and I think he gone with his
bent over sef but he's there again before I know it,
his eyes hard on my eyes whenever I look that way.
I don't know why he don't take his old sef somewhere
where he can do them old-timey dances with his
body rubbing its last rub, two-stepping with those
greased up ladies smelling like Avon.
Why he keep looking at me, all crazy like he know me,
his eyes on my dancin', dizzy like he dreamin' or
bout to black out? You know, I ain't messing with no
old man, even if he got money, no matter how hard
he look, and oh shit, here he come regular as
last call for alcohol, waddling over here with
them baggy old-time clothes and my friends
pushing me, go head dance with the old man, he
been watching, he been waiting all night, and
before I know it, I'm up and I'm movin' into
his curled arms, he's whispering just do it
like they used to, his breath thick with

whiskey but I listen, he moving like slow
water running, a rough cheek 'gainst my face,
his body shaking, mine needing to shake,
just do it like they used to, slow against me,
that last tavern dance, just like on Roosevelt,
he's seein' the blue light, hearing the
bluesman growl, thinking bout somebody harder,
somebody older, somebody loose and ready, smelling
like Avon, somebody who don't need bones to
just do it like they used to, move it like they used to.

All the while he was lookin', it was just
the movin' in me that mattered.
I was better than his last shot of booze.

He'll dream the good dream again tonight.
The one with music.

LIFE
ACCORDING
TO
MOTOWN

Oh, Mary Mac Mac Mac
All dressed in black, black, black
With silver buttons, buttons, buttons
All down her back, back, back.
She asked her mother, mother, mother
for fifteen cents, cents, cents
To see the elephant, elephant, elephant
Jump the fence, fence, fence.
He jumped so high, high, high
He touched the sky, sky, sky
And he didn't come back, back, back
Till the fourth of July, ly, ly.

        — Traditional children's clapping song

When I was nine years old,
growing tall tangled in bitter root,
I could whip my fingers numb with hand jive,
telling tall tales of rhythm and blue black superheroes
who only flew on Fridays
cause that's when the eagle flew.
My small hands put Mary Mac's buttons there,
the nickel and dime also glittered in my brown fist.
My flat singing hands grew red with a necessary music
as I heard my life blare from gaping westside windows.
Dressed in Motor City blues, even my pain was perfect pain.
Deep, deep, deep in the doo wop, I was a question
that you couldn't answer.

A thin layer of Vaseline and a thick pair of sweatsocks made your legs look bigger, made the muscles of your calves bulge. So when you jumped rope or when you just WALKED, the boys all came around, they sniffed at you like hot, hungry dogs, their pelvises just wouldn't sit still.

And you always had to make your hair look like more hair than it was. First you crammed the pores of your scalp with grease, then you flattened your hair with a pressing comb until it lay flat and black upside your head like ink. I was always trying to work a couple of rubberbands up on my little bit of hair, and the result could have been called pigtails — until the rubberbands popped off, that is.

If you lived on the west side of Chicago in the '60s and your hair was long and wavy and your skin was cream and your legs shone like glass, your ticket was as good as written.

But if you were truly bone black and your hair practically choked on its kinks, you waited for the music to give you a shape.

The Marvelettes made me pretty, Smokey wailed for just a little bit of me, and the Temptations taught me to wait, wait, wait for that perfect love.

Every two weeks, a new 45 hit the streets, but I already knew it, crying in my room under the weight of an imaginary lover, breathing steam onto mirrors, pretend slow dancing in the arms of a seriously fine young thang who rubbed at the small of my back with a sweet tenor.

In the real world the boys avoided me like creamed corn — but I was the supreme mistress of Motown, wise in the ways of love, pretending I knew why my blue jeans had begun to burn.

Those devils from Detroit were broiling my blood with the beat. They were teaching me that wanting meant waiting. They were teaching me what it meant to be a black girl.

WHAT IT'S LIKE TO BE A BLACK GIRL (FOR THOSE OF YOU WHO AREN'T)

● first of all, it's being 9 years old and
feeling like you're not finished, like your
edges are wild, like there's something,
everything, wrong. it's dropping food coloring
in your eyes to make them blue and suffering
their burn in silence. it's popping a bleached
white mophead over the kinks of your hair and
primping in front of mirrors that deny your
reflection. it's finding a space between your
legs, a disturbance at your chest, and not knowing
what to do with the whistles. it's jumping
double dutch until your legs pop, it's sweat
and vaseline and bullets, it's growing tall and
wearing a lot of white, it's smelling blood in
your breakfast, it's learning to say fuck with
grace but learning to fuck without it, it's
flame and fists and life according to motown,
it's finally having a man reach out for you
then caving in
around his fingers.

FIRST KISS

All previous attempts had failed miserably,
so I'd only dreamed of the sizzle
until Lloyd Johnson, a swaggering boy who breathed candy,
mashed me flat against the side of a Kedzie Ave. storefront.

I tried to kiss the way I thought Diana Ross would
(a dry, tight-lipped smack that hinted at so much more),
but this was nothing like the smooth, seamless smooches I'd
dreamed of.
This was a runaway bashing of throats, tongues and teeth,
this was a collision of misshapen mouths,
this was a feverish lip-tangling
that left my face feeling like the punchline to a bad joke.

So of course I fell in love,
which is what Motown said you did after someone kissed you.

Lloyd Johnson was having none of that, however.
He spoke to me in snickers from that moment on,
as if he'd ripped open a part of me
and didn't want to see what had spilled out.
He told everyone I wouldn't let him touch
what was shaking beneath my shirt,
he wouldn't let me call him boyfriend,
he wouldn't even let me call him Lloyd anymore.
Our faces never collided again.

Then everyone told me why.
It drives a boy crazy when he finds out
he's kissed a girl
no one has bothered to kiss before.

When the romance between Lloyd and Patricia began and ended with that one sloppy kiss, it took my daddy to slap a name on that heartbreak.

My daddy was a factory worker, worked at Leaf Candy Company on the west side of Chicago all his life, but nobody could tell me he didn't know about romance. He was short and skinny and almost bald, but you couldn't beat the ladies off him with a stick.

So I thought I was lucky because daddies teach little girls about little boys, that's just the way it is. But when daddy suddenly isn't around, you start waiting again. You wait for the music to give you a shape.

SWEET DADDY

62. you would have been 62.
i would have given you a roosevelt road kinda time,
an all-night jam in a twine time joint
where you could have taken over the mic
and crooned a couple

the place be all blue light
and jb air and big-legged women
giggling at the way you spit tobacco
into the sound system,
showing up some dime-store howler
with his pink car
pulled right up to the door outside

you would have been 62, and the smoke
would have bounced right off the top of your head
like good preaching
i can see you now, swirling those thin hips,
growling bout if it wudn't for bad luck,
you wudn't have no luck at all. i said
wudn't for bad luck
no luck at all

nobody ever accused you of walking
the paradise line
you could suck luckies
and line your mind with rubbing alcohol
if that's what the night called for,
but lord, you could cry foul
while bb growled lucille from the juke,
you could dance like killing roaches
and kiss those downsouth ladies
on fatback mouths. oooowweee, they'd say,
that sweet man sho knows how deep my well goes —
and i bet you did, daddy. i bet you did

but hey, here's to just another number,
to a man who wrote poems on the back of
cocktail napkins and brought them home
to his daughter who'd written her rhymes
under the cover of blankets
here's to a strain on the case load
here's to the fat bullet
that left its warm chamber to find you
here's to the miracles that spilled from your head
and melted into the air
like jazz

the carpet had to be destroyed. and your
collected works, on aging yellow twists of napkin

can't bring you back
bb wail and blue lucille

can't bring you back
a daughter who grew to write screams

can't bring you back. but a room
just like this one
that suddenly seems to fill with the dread odors
of whiskey and smoke
can bring you here, as close as breathing

but the moment is hollow.
it stinks.
it stinks sweet.

So Motown taught me all about men. Men worshipped women. Men couldn't live without women. The men who wailed beneath my phonograph needle were always begging you not to go, whining because you'd left after they'd begged you not to go, or praying out loud that you'd come on home so they could beg you not to go before you left them again.

But I remember my mother coming home from the taverns, dressed in sequins and Chanel, crying because the blues had broken through and touched bone, because she couldn't threaten to leave a man she didn't have.

I remember my friend Debra, her 11-year-old belly tight with the child of her mother's lover. She'd listened to the songs too, and waited along with me for the mindless drone of romance. She remembered him saying "I love you, I love you, really baby, I love you," and that's the way it was supposed to be, wasn't it, even in the movies wasn't it all sweet pain and shivering?

Debra told me she wasn't scared because babies just slipped out of your body while you were sleeping.

No men seemed to be begging my mother and Debra for anything. But I was still awkward, still skinny-legged, still wild by the head, still gawky and uncertain, still a stone fox when no one was around. I wanted so much to believe in the music.

So while the women I knew teetered, fell and crumbled in need of a beating heart, I kept waiting for a man to beg me for something.

It's not like I was asking for much
I didn't wanna be Diana, I just wanted to be Florence
the exact crooner in the background, the one with the hips
the one men winked at while shaking Diana's hand
the one who was so filled with heat and music
that one day her heart just burst instead of broke
I just wanted to be her

● There was a time I would have given a fine, light-skinned boy with curly hair several million dollars to simply look like he was about to think about thinking about asking me to dance.

That's what it was all about, a man who looked the way Motown sounded. He'd have the slickest edges. I only got to dance with the ones who sang a wet game in my ear or crooned off key into the side of my face, messing up the lyrics and wetting up my earlobes.

Those fine, "high yella" guys always made my body feel stupid. Lord, I'd see one of them every once in awhile and I'd gaze at him like he was ALL the answers. But the closest I'd come to dancing with one was when he stepped on my toe on the way to somebody else.

If you say Motown didn't teach you to slow dance, you're lying, pure and simple. Oh, you paler types may have done the tea parlor routine to Frankie Valli and the Four Seasons when your folks were around, but I know that as soon as they left you screwed the red bulb into the basement lamp and gave Smokey the rights to your body.

It was easy to pretend I was dancing with a boy everyone else wanted. All I had to do was put on "Ooh, Baby, Baby," wrap my hands around a pillow, bury my lips in it and move my feet real slow.

But pretty soon I had to realize that if I was 16 and waiting to dance, with my legs all greased up and my hair growing nappy under the hot lights, a real cute boy would be off somewhere else, breaking a more beautiful heart.

LAST DANCE

There is something wrong with my thighs tonight.
You have taught them lessons they shouldn't have learned.
Suddenly they are shores without water,
    slices of sun that warm nothing.
They are soft-skinned questions with the answer walking away.
You have taught them to curve and swoon around your fingers,
To strain and shake at the sound of your voice.

There is something wrong with my thighs tonight.
They have forgotten how to respond
to music.

Oh, Mary Mac
All dressed in black
With silver buttons
All down her back
She asked her mother
For fifteen cents
To see the elephant
Jump the fence
He jumped so high
He touched the sky
And he didn't come back